# Insight to the mind.

Ashleigh Briody

BookLeaf
Publishing

India | USA | UK

Presentation by *BookLeaf Publishing*

Web: www.bookleafpub.com

E-mail: info@bookleafpub.com

ISBN: 978-93-5744-959-5

First edition 2022

# DEDICATION

For Louise, Leo, Jennie, and Echo.


And especially my dad.

# ACKNOWLEDGEMENT

Thank you to my wonderful friends and family for always supporting my artistic side of expression through words, and not giving up on me.

# PREFACE

I saw the opportunity arise to take part in a poem-a-day for 21 days challenge and couldn't refuse this wonderful opportunity to show off my creative side and further enhance my writing skills.

# That's when I knew you were mine

You walked through my door with light in your
eyes and hope in your heart,
a passion for the unknown and a brand new start.
We played the piano and shared our laughter,
but nothing could ever prepare me for the days
that followed after.
A night of drinking where our friendship truly
started,
never guessing you and him could ever be
parted.
But lines were crossed and you knew what you
had to do,
you were unsure and fearful but you did what
was best for you.
Little did you know of the happiness you'd find,
and that's when I knew you were mine.

We drank our gin and beer whilst we talked the
night away,
we took a long stroll back to mine but you said
you couldn't stay.

Made sausages of crazy shapes with bread and
butter too,
took a picnic to the park whilst holding hands
like lovers do.
But we weren't together at this point we'd only
just begun,
if you'd known what I was truly like you'd have
only gone and run.
We talked and talked all day and night about our
struggles and our troubles,
as time went on things got much worse, all our
problems seemed to double.
No matter what was thrown our way things
always turned out fine,
and that's when I knew you were mine.

Over time my love for you only blossomed and
grew,
when you looked into my eyes and melted my
heart, that's when I knew.
That I had to make you my girl the one who I'd
first see when I wake,
to love and to cherish 'til death do us part and all
the memories that we'd make.
We've accomplished a lot in such little time with
us sharing a home and milestones passed,
first birthdays first Christmas first year as a
family, I'd be broken if someone said we
wouldn't last.

There's so many things still coming our way,
new house new home that's here to stay.
You love me and heal me even if I haven't a
dime,
and that's when I knew you were mine.


Before you came into my life I was lonely in
search of my soul mate,
you complete me profoundly with love and with
joy and it all comes down to our fate.
Your eyes your dimples your freckles and smile,
make the bad days and feuds more than
worthwhile.
Your hair and ears fulfil your look your beauty a
work of art,
I can't wait 'til the day that I'm saying I do, I
love you with all of my heart.
Never forget the warrior you are,
because, my love, you're a shooting star.
Our bond gets stronger time after time,
and that my dear is 'cause you are mine.

# My bonus child

Not mine by birth and not mine by law,
if I hadn't met your mother I wouldn't have
known you before.
Before your second birthday and before your
first word,
'you're not a real parent' I wish I never heard.

Not by features personality or blood,
but if you need me I'll be there, I would.
I'll hold your hand and guide you forever,
I only hope you realise how you've made my
life much better.

I wasn't there for your birth,
but let me tell you for all it's worth.
I'll see your first friendship first love and first
date,
my fiery determined red headed little mate.

I'll be your shoulder to cry on when you're
feeling down,
you'll never be alone 'cause you are loved all
around.
If there was a lottery of luck I'd have only gone
and won,

and if I could have chosen, you'd still be my
step son.

I love our little conversations they really make
my day,
reading books, catching balls and going out to
play.
Your sense of humour cracks me up it really
makes me laugh,
splashing, swimming, blowing bubbles, all
whilst in the bath.

Never lose that spark of yours 'cause that's what
makes you you,
you're brave and strong and full of fight, when I
saw you I just knew.
You'd fill the hole right in my heart as well as
mummy too,
no matter what life throws our way remember I
love you.

# A Gecko called Echo

I stare into your tank at night and watch you
come alive,
jumping high from branch to branch it's nice to
see you thrive.
Licking leaves, just as you do, once your home's
been sprayed,
not forgetting your eyeballs too, after all the
mess you've made.
You hide away all through the day but still I
know you're there,
I go to look for you again but I just don't know
where.
Disguised in branches leaves and soil, you're
such a happy soul,
if someone comes to take you out you'd hide or
dig a hole.
But you can't deny you love our cuddles, even if
you run,
or jump or fly or sprint or launch, my baby full
of fun.
I love your little kisses when you stick your
tongue right out,

climbing right up to my face to nudge me with
your snout.
When I bring you lively crickets, you can't
contain yourself,
fast as lightning snapping away, always full of
stealth.
You lighten up my life with your funny little
ways,
the joy you find in simple things, I'd watch you
play for days.
Your scaly skin and tiny toes, along with a little
tail,
makes me wonder what it's like each time you
inhale.
I don't know what I'd do without you, my baby I
call echo,
you make me feel proud everyday, even if
you're just a gecko.

# A baby to love all of my own

Ten little fingers and ten little toes,
a boy or a girl, nobody knows.
With bright beady eyes and a button nose,
a baby to love all of my own.

Will it have brown eyes, hazel, or blue,
will it look just like me or look just like you.
Will I still have these thoughts when you are all
grown,
a baby to love all of my own.

Your cute little face will light up a room,
we'll love you as far as the stars and the moon.
You'll melt any heart, like water from stone,
a baby to love all of my own.

I see mothers and babies of all different kinds,
and it hurts to wonder, when I will get mine.
So broody and desperate for a newborn to loan,
a baby to love all of my own.

You'll have a great brother who'll always be there,
he'll hold you and need you and love you, I swear.
For guidance and words in a lovingly tone,
a baby to love all of my own.

Two mamas of course to cater your needs,
double the love and double the feeds.
You'll be in our arms and complete our home,
a baby to love all of my own.

It'll be a long journey to bring you to life,
but with the help of a man, good luck, and my
wife.
Our dream will come true there'll be never a moan,
a baby to love all of my own.

Never forget just how loved you so are,
even if our meeting is ever so far.
When you are born I'll think, 'I've always known,
a baby to love, all of my own'.

# Teaching with a difference

A classroom with toys filled with tables and
chairs,
timetables, PECS books and help symbols too.
Learning all shapes such as circles and squares,
reading and writing and listening through.
All is quiet when the day has begun,
then we open the doors and start the day new.
In you all come with a thud as you run,
outside to play whilst the sky's still blue.

Some kids can talk and some kids cannot,
but all learn and grow at their own special pace.
Some kids have ear defs and chewies the lot,
no matter their needs I think they're all ace.
The laughter and giggles make hard days worth
while,
playing chase and catch and other games too.
Reading long stories to watch you all smile,
or cutting and drawing and sticking with glue.

Hearing first words and seeing new things,
makes us all so proud and tear up with joy.

Whether for food, toys, people or swings,
it's such an achievement for all to enjoy.
No matter your struggles when times get too
tough,
we'll guide you to safety and calm you right
down.
Loud noises bright lights, I know it seems rough,
we'll take care of it all there'll be never a frown.

Now the classroom's all silent the kids have
gone home,
time to tidy, plan, clean and set up.
What to explore tomorrow, the beads or the
foam,
learn how to dance, or drink from a cup.
My job may be stressful and difficult at times,
but there's something about it I just can't
explain.
I love teaching them numbers and nursery
rhymes,
back in the morning to do it all over again.

# What to eat?

Savoury, sour, tangy or sweet,
I think of these things when I'm ready to eat.
Shall I go to the fridge or look in the freezer,
that cake on the side is such a big teaser.

I turn on the oven, ready to cook,
think how is it done whilst I look at the book.
But my catering skills are not up to scratch,
compared to my dad, I know I'm no match.

So I turn off the oven start over again,
but my stomach is empty it's causing such pain,
Do I go for the crisps or the chocolate with nuts,
or place an order for tasty donuts.

Why do these questions flood out my head,
sometimes I give up and go back to bed.
But the hunger remains, so I head to the fridge,
I try some fresh fruit, but only a smidge.

Savoury, sour, tangy or sweet,
I think of these things when I'm ready to eat.
Can't make the decision, my mind filled with
dread,
I think I'll have McDonald's instead.

# Battlefield

Bodies laying on the floor with blood splattered open wounds,
expressions of shock lie upon their mucky lifeless faces.
Strips of blown up tattered uniform scattered along the ground,
beside missing limbs and exploded brains that coat the war torn soil.
Bullets ricochet off steel cap boots into the faces of our enemy,
with ammunition flying through the air like rays of light.
Bangs and booms of all dynamics, pitch and duration flood our ears,
rattling the ear drum with their powerful vibrations.
One man runs the outline of a mound praying for his peace,
but prying eyes with nifty vision spot his lonely presence.
Up comes the rifle with a newly changed magazine,
to obliterate the silhouette who wishes he'd followed the route.

Cuts and bruises overtake the bodies of the
innocent,
cries for forgiveness unheard through the sound
of war.
One last glance at the family portrait, before he
becomes their memory,
out into the battlefield to join his trusted platoon.
Retreat into the tunnel, our hearts pounding out
our chests,
section still intact for now, though scarred
throughout the trauma.
Shaking, screaming rocking too, the aftermath of
murder,
in the arms of each other, heads pressed together
as one.

# For my Nan

As I see some of your things,
the ones I've kept at mine.
Oh the memories that they bring,
it was such a better time.
A tea towel and a mug,
might seem like they're no big deal.
But they remind me of your hugs,
I hope, time will heal.
A plastic bin and babycham,
these things I hold so dear.
In my loft, they have been crammed,
to my eyes they bring a tear.
As I know these things in front of me,
are all that's left of you.
I wish that you were here to see,
you've left me feeling blue.
Of course it's not your fault,
it was just your time to go.
When your life came to a halt,
you were freed from pain, no more.
Every passing year from you,
I hope to make you proud.
I wonder if you think this too,
as I look up to the clouds.
I miss you so much everyday,

but now you are at peace.
I have just one thing that's left to say,
of my heart you have a piece.

# Snowy days

Snowflakes fall upon my cheeks,
as the colder days roll by.
White with winter ever so bleak,
this cold and frosty sky.
The clouds and sky merge into one,
can not be told apart.
A wonderland that's free from sun,
a magical work of art.
The snow builds up onto the ground,
thicker by the minute.
Softly fall without a sound,
pushing beauty to its limit.
That frosty feeling coats my face,
turns my skin a nice bright red.
I take it in with all its grace,
through my cold and frozen head.
Icicles that pave the house,
and footprints from a bird.
Frozen taps no good to douse,
its water cannot be stirred.
These days are all but rare,
but when they do come it shows.
Watch the children stop and stare,
how they love it when it snows.

# What music means to me

One feeling that I can't describe is what music
means to me,
no matter the situation, no matter the time of
day,
music seems to speak for me when I've nothing
else to say.
It's boosts the mood with throw back vibes,
playing songs from the eighties,
relatable lyrics through nineties hits, get me
through the week.
Any genre, any length, it doesn't matter to me,
as I listen between the lines and feel what's truly
underneath.
Every song has a story, be it sad or filled with
joy,
words of wisdom sang through gritted teeth.
Holding back their true emotions to make it
through the song,
knowing only of their struggles that lie beneath.
Radiating blissful peace, my favourite indie
playlist,

helping me to get some rest, and ease my
wandering mind.
Good for any time of day, it helps to heal my
soul,
a song can guide you past bad thoughts, or help
to soothe your heart.

# Black and white

Dark thoughts, lonely nights,
early mornings and loss of light.

Overthinking, over-stressed,
maybe I'm just simply depressed?

The feeling's taking over, much more than it
seems,
some dream of hope, some, hanging from
beams.

Lost, numb, gone and cold,
should I really have these feelings when I'm
only this old?

A hug to heal the body, words to soothe the
mind,
a kiss to ease the shakes, a calm voice to remind.

Remind me that I shouldn't worry, it's all just in
my head,
would they still think that if they found me
dead?

But I refuse the hugs and ignore the words,
I pity the kisses, and never feel heard….

Dramatic, selfish, annoying and weird,
am I really one to be feared?

All I want is acceptance, all I want is love,
an understanding friend, a sign from above.

That things will get better, that things will be
okay,
that I am not alone, a reason to stay.

Sickness of the body, always treated with
concern,
but sickness of the mind and they leave you out
to burn.

It controls your life, chooses the world you see,
I'm not overreacting, I  have BPD.

# Going on holiday

The drive up to the airport always fills my heart
with joy,
even as a kid I'd smile and hold my favourite
toy.
The busy lanes and worn out faces paint the
stressful scene,
children screaming with excitement, parents not
so keen.
As they know the pain of queues and lines, the
never ending scans,
hours later sitting nicely, tickets in their hands.

The plane takes off with a crash, vacation set in
motion,
as I look outside the window, I see the deepest
purest ocean.
Mini bar and meals on wheels come flying down
the aisle,
children asking 'are we there yet', for each
passing mile.
The long and gruelling wait is over people piling
off the plane,
I see long walk ways with windows, all held up
by a crane.

The sweet smell of heat fills my nose as I
breathe,
I take off my jacket as my blood starts to seethe.
As we crowd onto the coach, our holiday begins,
cannot contain my excitement, as if I'm sitting
on pins.
A tall white building surrounded by trees stands
in front,
off the coach and for our suitcases, we start the
hunt.

Cocktail in hand as I lay in the sun,
I see families and friends having all kinds of fun.
Roasting away getting browner by the second,
by the smell of foreign food, my nose beckons.
Pizzas with sausage and fancy meat too,
I know when I leave, I'll be left feeling blue.

Swimming in the pool at night that's lit up all
around,
the moon's reflection in the water, speaks of
peace I've finally found.
Lively night life, melting ice cream, sunny
tourist spots,
eating lays in hotel rooms and downing loads of
shots.
People all around the world, crave their week of
bliss,

a break from reality once a year, so hard not to miss.

# Keep trying

When things get tough and seem to fail,
you must keep trying no matter what.
At least that's everyone's favourite tale,
'be grateful for the things you've got'.

But it's not as simply as it seems,
your mind can be a scary place.
'Just don't be sad' ha, in your dreams,
if that was true then I'd feel ace.

But getting help may be the fix,
that one voice that you know you'll trust.
At first your feelings may be a mix,
soon turns your worries into dust.

Relationships build over time,
it does not happen overnight.
Can sometimes feel like it's a crime,
to drag your loved ones into light.

They can help you with your daunting past,
or problems that are  present.
And soon you'll feel relief at last,
a mindset now so pleasant.

When things get tough and seem to fail,
You must keep trying, no matter what.
Even if you try to no avail,
Don't give up, give your best shot.

# My mate Jen

Ten years of friendship and you are still here,
been through thick and through thin, to me you
are dear.
With our perfume and yoghurts we'd laugh 'til
we dropped,
funny accents, impressions, we never should
have stopped.

With time we grew up but never apart,
new jobs and new lives and a brand new start.
Though these things couldn't break away our
bond,
sunbathing, eye spy and smoking by the pond.

Jen you're my rock and my shoulder to cry on,
you've picked me back up, when all hope was
gone.
Without your love and faith, and words of truth,
I'd be totally different, a wasted youth.

Never lose  that fiery spark,
through your courage, you're my light in the
dark.
Although distance between us is something
that's new,
always remember, that I love you.

. . .

28

It's thick and fulfilling and loaded with fun,
can be used by your dad or used by your mum.
Easy to buy and easy to get,
once you see it your mind will be set.
You can open it up and close it again,
but don't get it wet 'cause it might leave a stain.
All different shapes and all different sizes,
if you reach its end you feel it's prizes.
It can fill you with spunk and help you to cook,
it's not what you think, it's only a book!

# Isolated

You'll never know what it's like to be the last
one chosen,
The one who no one wants to walk beside, and
always trails behind.
Lonely pacing with no room left, feeling nothing
but frozen,
When questioned by the others, I simply say I do
not mind.

Watching as they plan their party, hoping I'd be
busy,
Not daring to mention it to me, in fear I'd have
to come.
But they needn't worry about me, as I'd just say
I was dizzy,
And stay at home alone and sad, well and truly
done.

Treated different from the rest, I sit and moon
alone,
No one even seems to notice the absence of my
presence.
They slate me hate me scorn me, and say all I do
is moan,

But how could I feel any other way, than this
lonely worthless adolescent.

I sometimes stop and wonder, why I join them
all the time,
But the thought of having no one really worries
me so sick.
So I put up with the name calling, the jokes as
sour as lime,
You're stupid annoying we don't like you, god
you are so thick.

I knew I couldn't go on like this, I'd truly had
enough,
I had to face my fears and make my voice
thoroughly heard.
I stood my ground about the abuse, even though
it was so tough,
So as I let them go and started afresh, I felt I had
been cured.

# Clouds

I sit and watch the day go by outside my
bedroom window.
As I look up in the sky I see the rolling clouds
go by.
I wonder where they're going, I think about their
journey.
Their colours and shapes collide into one,
making new formations.
A big gust of wind appears and speeds them on
their way.
What was once a star now becomes a tree, big
clouds turn to small clouds,
and small clouds come as one.
The sun shines through the middle, parting like
the sea.
Big rays of sunlight fill the sky, with colours
dancing all around.
The clouds are on their way now, as the sun
starts taking over.
Fading away into the summer sky they disappear
once more.

# Being gay

Struggling to find someone, not knowing where
to look,
dating sites and applications, a chance I could
have taken.
Awkward meetings late at night, not knowing
what to say,
but it's not that hard, you're only gay?

Catfishes online, with fake profiles and fake
names,
being strung along and made to believe, they
play their little games.
But when you actually find someone, you
wonder if they'll stay,
but it's not that hard, you're only gay?

Holding hands in public, with my fiancée's
always tough,
we get dirty looks and comments made, will it
always be this rough?
God forbid we have a kiss, we'd be societies
prey,
but it's not that hard, you're only gay?

Telling family of your secret, can go one way or
the other,
some may be accepting, some may blame it on
your mother.
Could be kicked out to the curb or made to
always stay,
but it's not that hard, you're only gay?

The world sees our community, but doesn't
change its ways,
everything's for 'man and woman', it makes us
feel astray.
Anniversary cards for queers, ha, what a price
we pay,
but it's not that hard, you're only gay?

Of course it's not all negative, there's
somethings I wouldn't change,
festivals of pride and love, to others, may seem
strange.
Putting rainbows onto everything, is just our
special way,
i'm so glad to be me and proud to say I'm gay!

# I miss you

I miss you.
I miss your loving nature and drive for life,
your lust for adventure at any waking moment.
You could walk and run and jump for miles,
but never hesitated when called to be right by
my side.

I miss you.
I miss your companionship and patience,
your cuddles and your kisses.
The time you'd spend just laying by my side,
letting me stroke you and hold you and play with
your ears.

I miss you.
I miss the joy you'd feel through such simple
things,
a ball or a toy or attention from others.
A course of agility or a swim in a pond,
a happy little soul you were.

I miss you.
I may not have been your true owner,
but you owned me with your heart of gold.
May have been 'just a dog' to others,
but to me you were my first furry love.

# Our Pride

On the road and on our way, to our very first
pride,
we ate some food and sang some songs with
pure excitement.
The wind in our hair and hope in our soul, was
such a joyful ride,
soon enough we pulled into the inn, to prepare
for the event.
The atmosphere was magical, it's such a sight to
see,
streets plastered with rainbow flags, with colours
everywhere.
Back again to where I feel home, totally free to
be me,
and her first time with me by her side, truly the
perfect pair.

Browsing the stalls along with the food, soaking
up the vibes,
we drank and danced and sang and laughed,
until the night was through.
The gays and queers and lesbians too, danced
swiftly in their tribes,
friendly faces nevertheless loved, being there
was a dream come true.

Back to the inn to get ready again, for the nights
delights,
make up redone and an outfit change, we set off
on our way.
Beaming lights and disco vibes, it's such a
beautiful sight,
love and acceptance with never a worry, I only
wish we'd stay.

But the second night was where it all changed,
she gave my life true meaning,
as I sat on the bed in our hotel room, I saw her
open a box.
She took my hand and spoke her words, my face
utterly beaming,
finally my fiancée of natural beauty and long
wavy locks.
The live music that followed after, was our
nights celebration,
my heart felt full, my smile was illuminating, I
couldn't hide my emotions.
I love this girl with all my being, the luckiest
one in the nation,
for her I'd give up everything, and swim in the
deepest of oceans.

A spa filled with saunas and a pool to unwind, is
where we ventured next,

to make our weekend complete, and pamper
ourselves silly.
Ever so relaxed and ever so peaceful, we felt its
full effects,
tried some new food on our sweet little date, and
laughed involuntarily.
Memories of our first pride will stay with me
forever,
a time of happiness within our means, and new
milestones hit.
Your presence like a warming hug, I'd go with
you wherever,
you are my missing puzzle piece, with me you
surely fit.

# Taking it all in

A low flying bird takes to the sky, swooping its
way past,
its small body of crimson red, is no match for its
soaring black wings.
Fast as lightning it glides through the air,
looking for something to do,
spots a worm of innocent nature, and swoops
again no more.

Light winds creep in to the midday weather,
taking the leaves as it blows,
accompanied with clouds and a touch of frost,
making my breath a visual treat.
It ripples the water and hurries the litter, all
along the grassy terrain,
and my goosebumps it heightens, with many
hairs standing on end.

Although mostly silent, there can be some slight
sounds detected,
the tweets of the bird with the worm in its
mouth, perched lightly on a branch.
Rustling leaves that crinkle and scrape, with
growing waves behind,

forceful wind calls that start to pick up, a sign
that winter is coming.

Nature's scents complete the scene, an
atmosphere of heaven,
grass and frost and wildlife too, these smells
maintain the memory.
A gift from earth too pure for most humans, puts
reality in its place,
this break from all stress and burdens of life, is
ever so easy to reach.

www.ingramcontent.com/pod-product-compliance
Lightning Source LLC
LaVergne TN
LVHW021311200726
843509LV00012B/1869